TRIMMING AND CLIPPING

by

Valerie Watson

Illustrations by

Carole Vincer

KENILWORTH PRESS

Copyright © 1986 The Kenilworth Press Ltd

First published in the UK in 1986
by Kenilworth Press, an imprint of Quiller Publishing Ltd

Reprinted 1987, 1988, 1990, 1991, 1993, 1994
Second edition 1999
Reprinted 2003, 2005, 2008, 2010

British Library Cataloguing-in-Publication Data
A catalogue record for this book
is available from the British Library

ISBN 978 1 872119 23 6

Printed in China

Kenilworth Press
An imprint of Quiller Publishing Ltd
Wykey House, Wykey, Shrewsbury, SY4 1JA
Tel: 01939 261616 Fax: 01939 261606
E-mail: info@quillerbooks.com
Website: www.kenilworthpress.com

CONTENTS ■ ■ ■ ■ ■ ■ ■ ■ ■ ■ ■ ■ ■

TRIMMING AND
CLIPPING

Introduction

When we trim and clip horses and ponies we are interfering with nature. Horses and ponies grow heavy coats to keep them warm and dry in winter. Some grow thick feather on their legs and long coarse hairs on their jaws to protect them from wet and muddy conditions while grazing. In summer the long wispy hairs that grow on their heads keep flies and other insects at bay.

A horse's appearance can be dramatically improved if he is trimmed, but his well-being must come first. Trim him only if he is able to find shelter from flies and from bad weather. Ponies who compete in native breed classes are usually shown untrimmed.

Clipping off the winter coat is a step which should not be taken without due thought and preparation. Unless the animal is a hardy type and is given only a very low trace clip he will need to be stabled at night, and must wear rugs to replace nature's thermal clothing. A horse grows two coats every year: a summer coat in spring and a winter coat during the autumn. Therefore if you clip off his winter coat your horse will not grow a replacement, although periodical re-clipping will be necessary to remove the thin, untidy growth of hair which will appear.

Looking after a clipped, stabled horse takes up a lot of time. You will need to allow several hours a day to exercise him, groom him and muck out his stable. He must be fed regularly. But it will all be worth it, and your reward will be the pleasure of riding a horse who is able to work well and easily on a cold winter's day.

When it comes to clipping and trimming, there is no substitute for experience. It is easy to work with scissors and clippers, but not so easy to do it well. Those who are able to clip and turn out a horse or pony to perfection have reason to be proud.

'BEFORE'   'AFTER'

Trimming the head

The lines of a fine head can be accentuated and the looks of a coarse head improved by trimming the long hairs which grow on a horse's jaws, muzzle and ears.

Always trim gently, to the level of the coat, **using scissors with rounded ends.**

The jaws: To begin, remove the headcollar and put it around the horse's neck, with the noseband facing back. Unless the horse is very quiet, an assistant should hold him. When you have finished, the jawline and the hollow between the jaws should look smooth and natural. Cutting too deeply into the coat can leave ugly 'steps'. Always trim a little at a time.

The muzzle: Some people leave the muzzle whiskers long, because they act as feelers. It is a matter of opinion as to whether they are trimmed completely or not at all. If you trim them, do it only with scissors, all round the muzzle and nose. Do not trim the whiskers around the eyes – without them the horse's eyes could be badly injured.

The ears: The hairs which grow inside the ear act as a barrier to insects and draughts. On no account should they be removed. It is, however, reasonable to trim round the edges and on the flat borders just inside the ears, to make them more shapely (see illustrations on page 6). Work quietly, with an assistant to hold the horse. Some horses will be more relaxed if they cannot see what you are doing. The assistant can bring this about by gently placing a cupped hand behind the horse's eye to block his sight, like a blinker.

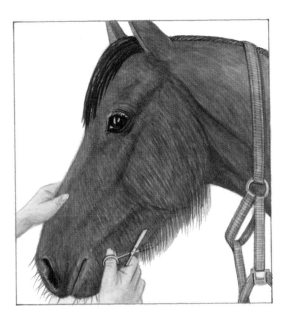

1. Long, fine hairs grow around the jaw bones and the hollow between them. Trim these long cat hairs away, taking care not to cut too deeply into the coat.

2. Then use your scissors above a comb to make a smooth finish. Work from the chin groove to the throat. Also trim the hairs on the cheeks and the muzzle.

Trimming the ears

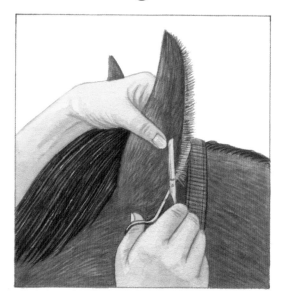

1. Hold the ear gently in the left hand. Squeeze the edges together so that the excess hair stands out. Trim this hair away gently, close to the edges of the ear.

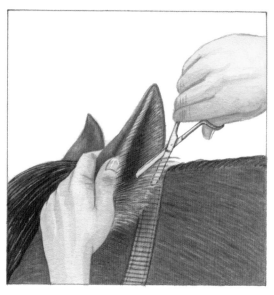

2. Open the ear out carefully and hold it still with the left hand. Trim the long hairs, from the tip to the broadest part of the ear. Trim round the edge.

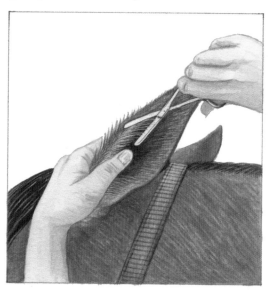

3. Trim the excess hair from the front edge. Horses are sensitive here, so be gentle. The hairs in and around the edge of the ear will now be short and even.

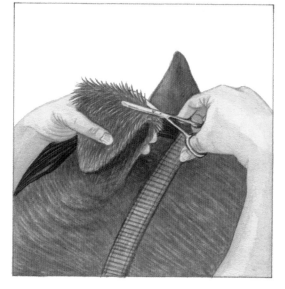

4. Fold the ear over to trim any long 'cat' hairs which may be visible. Now trim the other ear. Finally, brush out both ears gently. Make sure that they look the same.

Trimming the legs

In summer you can improve your horse's looks by trimming his feather, heels and coronets. This will make his legs look finer. If the horse or pony is living outdoors through the winter, it is kinder to leave his legs hairy, because in wet conditions the water drains straight down the long feather to the ground; the soft flexible parts at the back of the pasterns and in the heels, which lie under the feather, remain dry.

The shaggier the legs, the more difficult they will be to trim. If you cut too deeply into the coat in one place, and less deeply in another, you will create ugly 'steps' up the back of your horse's legs. While trimming, squat in a balanced way so that you can move quickly to avoid the horse's legs if he moves or kicks. Follow the procedure shown in the diagrams. After successful trimming, the legs should look completely natural, as if they have always been feather-free and have never seen a pair of scissors.

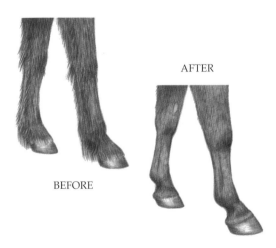

AFTER

BEFORE

Horses competing in winter should have clean and tidy legs. Untrimmed legs can be more prone to mud-fever and wounds more difficult to spot.

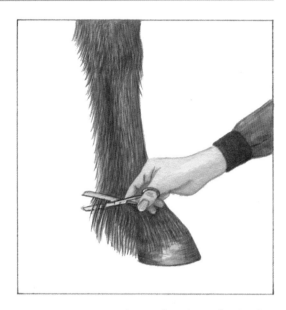

1. Cut off most of the feather from the back of the fetlock and pastern. Leave 3cm (1.25ins) of hair so that you can shape round the fetlock joint later.

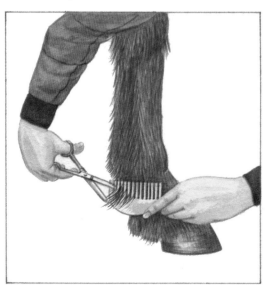

2. Comb up the back of the pastern. As the comb fills with hair, stop and trim the hair showing through the teeth until all the hair from heel to ergot is short.

Trimming the legs cont.

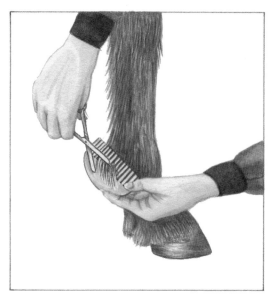

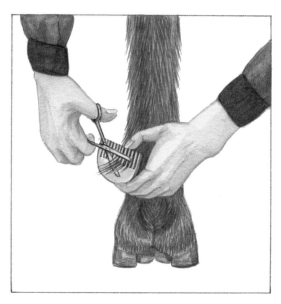

3. Using comb and scissors as before, trim the outside of the fetlock. Work from the ergot round the joint, leaving a smooth natural-looking finish.

4. Repeat the method on the inside of the fetlock, working from the ergot around the joint. Comb and trim little by little, to reveal the fetlock's shape.

5. Use comb and scissors to trim any long hairs from the back of the tendons. Leave a smooth finish with no ugly 'steps' in the hair.

6. Thick hair above the front of the coronet may be thinned with comb and scissors. Finally, cut a level edge, just below the coronet band.

Clipping considered

Clipping is the term used for shaving away the horse's coat with a clipping machine.

The choice of clip should be geared to the individual needs of the horse, the kind of work he is doing, and your stable management system. The traditional types of clip are the **full clip**, the **hunter clip**, the **blanket clip** and the **trace clip**.

If a horse is stabled at night and works hard regularly during the winter it is sensible to remove some or all of his winter coat. For the best results, wait until the coat is 'set' or fully grown before clipping. This is usually some time in October.

Reasons for clipping
• To enable the animal to work hard without the extra stress which a heavy coat would cause.
• To reduce sweating, thus helping to maintain condition.
• To prevent chills. Heavy coats hold the sweat, and they dry slowly in cold weather.
• The horse will be easier to keep clean and will look smarter.
• For medical reasons. A small area may be clipped to keep a wound clean and to help treatment.

Do **not** clip until you have considered the following:
1. Horses can do light work in reasonable comfort without being clipped.
2. You will need to buy or borrow a clipping machine.
3. Getting a novice horse used to the machine will take time and patience (see page 12).
4. You will need an experienced assistant (or two if the horse is nervous) to help with the clipping.

5. The horse may need re-clipping every two or three weeks.
6. The clipped horse will need a lot of attention every day. He must be fed, exercised and groomed regularly. You will also need to keep a wary eye out for any chafing caused by girths, rubber reins, etc.
7. Horses who are full, hunter, blanket or chaser clipped must be stabled at night and must wear rugs, night and day. You will need extra clothing as follows: a warm night rug • a warm under-rug or two blankets • a wither pad and roller • an anti-sweat rug, for use after exercise, for travelling and for extra warmth in very cold conditions • a quarter sheet or day rug, for use while on exercise • a New Zealand rug, for turning out • and for the fully clipped horse, a set of stable bandages or leg wraps, to increase warmth and circulation in cold conditions. Grass-kept ponies, even with minimal clips, usually need a New Zealand – ideally two. Use common sense and keep an eye on the pony's condition and the weather.

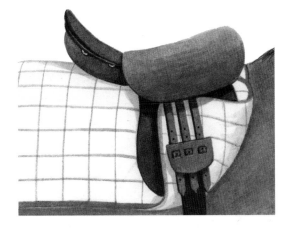

When using a quarter sheet, fold it back and underneath the girth straps to prevent it slipping back during exercise.

How to clip

Learning to clip

If possible, watch a professional in action so that you have a fair idea of what's involved. Before you start on your own horse or pony, ask an experienced person to show you how to begin and, if possible, get a little hands-on experience on a placid horse. And remember, if you do make a mistake, the coat will always grow back again!

Where to do the clipping

• Work in a safe, quiet, enclosed place, preferably outside.
• For clipping, a power point for the machine must be near by. Trailing wires should be avoided.
• Never clip outside in wet conditions. Make sure that you and your horse are standing on a dry surface.
• If clipping in a stable, sweep back the bedding. It will then be easier to clear up afterwards. Remove the water bucket. The less metal and water in the vicinity, the better.
• Some people have special clipping boxes with floors covered in rubber matting, and with special artificial lighting. These are extremely useful when the weather is too wet for you to work outside.
• Feed a haynet. It helps the horse to pass the time away.

Useful tips

• Dress for comfort and safety. A smock or overall, fastened at the neck, will protect you from irritating hairs. Do not wear wool, as the loose hair will cling to it. Tie back your hair if necessary, and cover it. A hard hat is a good idea, especially for nervous horses.
• Your footwear should give some protection. Rubber soles are essential for clipping.
• Progress with the job quietly and patiently. Never hurry when trimming or clipping. Allow plenty of time – at least three hours for most types of clip.
• Clip when the light is good. Start clipping in the morning. In autumn the afternoons grow cold and the light fades quickly. Natural light is best.
• Be aware of how much hair the clippers can manage. If you try to cut or clip too much at once the hair will be pulled. Most of the horses who are shy of clippers have at some time or another been cut, poked, or hurt by blades that pull.
• Remember that horses who have never been hurt or frightened by the experience, usually enjoy being trimmed or clipped as much as they enjoy being groomed.

Draw out your clipping lines with chalk or soap before you begin. Check that the patterns are the same on both sides. A piece of string serves as a useful measuring device.

Getting started

On the day before clipping, give your horse a long exercise. Do not ride him just before clipping because you cannot clip a sweaty coat. Groom him thoroughly – a clean coat is easier to clip well. Mark out the clipping lines carefully, using chalk or soap. Prepare the machine. Make a trial clip under the neck to check that the machine is working properly. The blades should glide through the coat, cutting the hairs easily. You should not need to force them. If the machine is not clipping easily, stop immediately, as blades which pull will hurt the horse.

The machine may be labouring for one of the following reasons: (a) incorrect tension; (b) blunt blades; (c) the wrong type of blades for the coat. Make the required alterations.

• Always clip against the lay of the coat. How to tackle difficult areas, where the coat grows in various ways, is shown in the diagrams.

• Work along the horse's body from front to rear, clipping in small sections and covering the finished area of his back with a rug.

• Progress each section by clipping a strip and then a parallel strip above or below it. Each strip should slightly overlap the preceding one, so the blades seldom have a complete width of hair to clip.

• Keep the blades flat. If you clip with them at an angle towards the skin, you could cut the horse and leave deep clipping lines. Keep the pressure even.

• When clipping a thick coat, go over the same area two or three times, going deeper into the coat each time.

• Test the bottom of the blades frequently. Stop to let them cool **before** they become uncomfortably hot for the horse. While they cool, check your work. Note any parts you have missed or which need tidying up.

• It doesn't hurt to give yourself and your horse a break during a clipping session. Loose him, adequately rugged, in a stable, where he can drink and stale.

• Horses are sensitive on their heads, under their bellies and inside the tops of their legs. Clip these parts while the blades are cool.

• The hair on the throat, between the front legs, and under the stifle, is difficult to reach. Using your free hand, gently stretch the skin over a flat piece of bone or flesh, to make it accessible to the clippers. Take care not to nick the skin. If you do, the horse will not appreciate that area being clipped again.

Clipping a straight line. Carefully run the clippers along the line marked by the chalk.

Forgetting to overlap your clipping lines, will not give your clip a smooth finish.

You can tidy an edge by holding the clippers sideways-on. Or you can trim untidy edges by holding the clippers vertically and lifting them through the hair. However, this second method requires a skilful hand and a very still horse!

How to clip cont.

The assistant's tasks
• To hold and reassure a young or nervous horse, and distract the horse while critical or tricky areas are clipped.
• To pick up and stretch out each front leg while the elbow and the inside of the forearm are clipped. The leg should be held by the hoof or fetlock, never by the tendons. See page 16.
• To stop the horse moving by holding up a front leg. (This is particularly useful when clipping the legs of a fidgety horse.) The assistant should stand in a well-balanced way with his feet apart. He should hold the hoof in one hand and support the knee with the other – see page 16. When working on a hind leg, the front leg on the same side should be held up, as horses can kick while standing on diagonal legs.
• To help with the head by holding and soothing the horse. If necessary, his view can be screened with a cupped hand at the back of his eye, like a blinker. Some parts of the head are easier to clip if the headcollar is removed and fastened round the neck with the noseband facing back.
• If all else fails, to apply and hold a twitch while the final sensitive areas **are quickly clipped.**

Preparing a young or nervous horse, or clipping a first-timer
Plan to spend ten minutes each day for a week accustoming your horse to the sound and vibration of the clipping machine. First, run the machine or a tape recording of it, near to him. Then show him the machine while it is turned off. Let him smell it. Stroke him with it. Do not frighten him with the cable. Pat him and reward him, so that he associates the machine with pleasure. If another horse is being clipped, let him watch.

Accustoming a novice horse to the vibration of a clipping machine.

To accustom the horse to the vibration, place your hand, palm down, on the horse's body – say, on his shoulder – and rest the running clippers on the back of your hand. Progress to stroking him with the body of the machine while it is turned on. The machine should become as familiar to him as his body brush. If possible, don't make his first clip a full one; opt for a light trace clip of some kind. That way he should be fairly relaxed when you clip him next time.

Sedation
If your horse simply will not tolerate clipping, ask your vet to prescribe a suitable sedative. Sometimes this works, but not always. However, to keep you and your horse safe it is worth trying once.

After clipping
When finished, groom your horse well and rug him up. If he is unsettled, lead him out for a nibble of grass. Sweep up the clipped hair. Put it in a bag in the dustbin. It will not rot on the muck heap.

The clipping machine

There are several types of clipping machine. Electric clippers are the most common and should always be used in conjunction with a circuit-breaker for safer clipping. You can also buy rechargeable clippers (with no trailing wires) and others which are powered from a battery pack strapped to the user's waist (involving just a short wire from waist to hand). In addition there are slimline hand-held battery or rechargeable clippers for trimming the head and around sensitive areas; these are not suitable for clipping the whole coat.

Before clipping, see that the cable, plug and circuit-breaker are in good condition or ask an electrician to check them. Follow the maker's instructions as to which blades to use and how to fit them – fine or medium are best for most horses. Check that the machine is clean, oiled and in good running order. Oil, then wipe the teeth while the machine runs. Screw the tension nut up tight, then back **one and a half turns**. If the machine sounds too low and laboured, the nut is too tight. If the noise is high and fast, and if the blades rattle, it is too loose.

When clipping, do not let the horse chew or stand on the cable.

Clean and oil the blades frequently while clipping, and brush the hair away from the blade head and any air filters. Check that the blades do not overheat. If they do, stop to let them cool.

After clipping, brush the machine thoroughly. Clear the air filter. Dismantle and clean the head. Clean the blades. If you need to prevent infection, wash them in a mild disinfectant. Dry them thoroughly. Store the machine in a dry place, with the blades unattached.

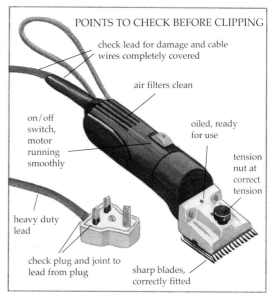

POINTS TO CHECK BEFORE CLIPPING

check lead for damage and cable wires completely covered

air filters clean

on/off switch, motor running smoothly

oiled, ready for use

tension nut at correct tension

heavy duty lead

check plug and joint to lead from plug

sharp blades, correctly fitted

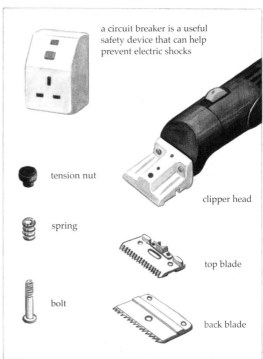

a circuit breaker is a useful safety device that can help prevent electric shocks

tension nut

spring

bolt

clipper head

top blade

back blade

Clippers and parts should be kept clean and dry. Good maintenance of your clippers is essential.

The full clip

The full clip is used on horses and ponies who are expected to work hard or compete regularly in show classes during the winter. Animals with coarse coats are sometimes clipped out during the summer, to reduce sweating. Hunters are often full clipped in the autumn and hunter-clipped in November. This way the clipped legs look smart and are easy to keep clean, but a little hair will grow back to give some protection. The full clip entails removing all of the coat except for a small triangle above the tail and a very narrow strip just below the root of the mane, widening around the withers.

Before deciding to full clip, make sure you have sufficient warm rugs. Make sure that they are in good condition and that they fit the horse.

When clipping, work from the front towards the rear, unfolding a rug over the

THE FULL CLIP

1. To begin, turn the machine on and start clipping here. Lie the head of the machine flat on the coat and begin to clip slowly against the growth of the hair.

2. Clipping the mane line. Brush the mane over to the other side. Clip along the top of the neck 1cm (0.5ins) below the roots of the mane. Leave a neat, continuous line.

finished area as you work.

After the body, clip the legs. Clip against the lie of the coat but work down each leg in sections. Clip outwards from the ergot. Hold up each leg to clip the back of the pastern and the coronet.

Lastly, clip the head as shown on page 17. The blades must be cool. Be very patient and careful. Given time and perseverance you will probably be able to clip the whole head without using a twitch. However, if the horse will not tolerate the clippers near parts of his head, apply a twitch to his upper lip. You will need an experienced assistant. **Never apply a twitch to an ear or lower lip.** Once the twitch is on, complete your task carefully and quickly. Remove it as soon as you have finished. Encourage the horse to rub his nose, to restore circulation.

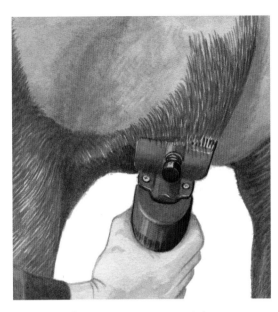

Between the front legs is one of the most difficult places to clip. Take care not to nick the horse in this area.

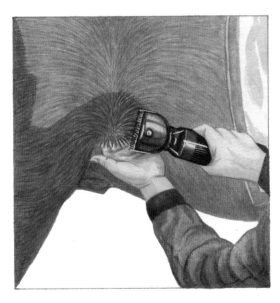

3. From stifle to hip. Here the hair grows in a fan shape. Clip against the growth, in half circles. Expose the tender skin from under the stifle, as shown. Clip it carefully.

4. Clipping the rump. A rug covers the back and loins which have been clipped. Clipping the rump is fun but the clipping lines show up, so take care to keep the pressure even.

The full clip cont.

5. Leaving a triangle above the tail. Cut a line about 15cm (6 in.) long from each side of the tail to the centre of spine to make a neat isosceles triangle.

6. Clipping the elbow. Ask someone to hold the leg forward to stretch the soft folds of skin which are otherwise easily nicked. Your free hand can ease the skin to make it accessible.

7. To preventing fidgeting and kicking, a front leg can be held up, supported under knee and hoof. Here the horse will have difficulty moving his off fore and near hind.

8. Clipping the inside of a hind leg. It is sometimes easier to do this from the other side. Detect and deter any movement by holding the tail and the hamstring. Keep alert!

9. Clip from chin groove to throat. (Throat hairs grow in various ways on floppy skin.) Next do the cheeks. Clip lightly over bony parts to reduce vibration.

10. Now clip the front of the head, starting between the nostrils. Finish at the whorls of hair on the forehead. Carefully clip the cheek bones and under the eyes.

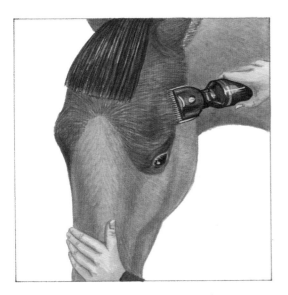

11. Next clip the forehead, above the eyes and round the base of the ears. Mind the forelock! The hollows over the eyes can be tricky to do, so take extra care.

12. Clip the ears last. Adapt the method shown on page 6. If you can't easily reach the ears without stretching, stand on a box. You may need a twitch, fitted as here.

The hunter clip

Hunters work hard for long hours. They need to be clipped but their legs are vulnerable to thorns and knocks and their backs may become sore when they are ridden all day. The hunter clip involves clipping the body and head, as with the full clip, but the legs and a saddle patch are left unclipped. The saddle patch acts as a natural numnah; it should be the same shape on both sides of the horse and level at the spine and on both sides of the withers.

To outline a saddle patch, first put the saddle on, without its fittings, and slide it into its natural position (a saddle patch in the wrong place looks terrible). Draw round the saddle with chalk, then either remove it and clip round the area you have marked, or fit the girths and clip round the saddle, removing it to finish off.

THE HUNTER CLIP – named after the animal to which it is best suited. When the horse is tacked up, a thin strip of hair will be visible around the edge of the saddle.

Clipping around the saddle. Clip the neck. Then start to clip around the saddle. Leave a broad band of hair showing, to allow for mistakes. Now tidy the edges of the patch.

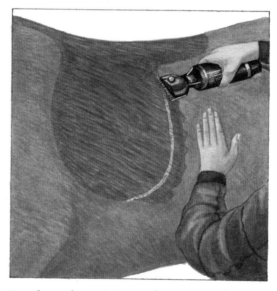

Finishing the saddle patch. To make the line at the back smooth, not ragged, clip into the hair slowly, then slide the machine back out of it. Work down the line with short strokes.

To begin with, make the saddle patch a little larger than you intend it to be finally, to allow for mistakes when you are tidying up the edges.

The leg lines should slope on the insides and outsides of the legs, as shown. Near the front of each leg there should be an inverted V, and round the back a gentle curve. Mark out the lines with chalk, using the width of your hand to gauge their positions. As a rough guide:

• On the front legs, make the point of the V one hand's width from where the leg joins the chest. Make the curve two widths below the elbow.

• On the hind legs, make the point of the V four widths below the top of the stifle and the curve two widths above the point of the hock. The points of the Vs on the forearms must be level, as should the curves round the back of the hind legs.

For extra protection of the face, or a first-time clip, you can leave half the head unclipped. Follow the line of the bridle cheekpiece and extend down to the muzzle.

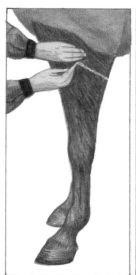
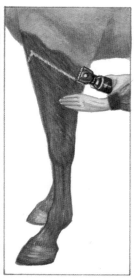

Marking and clipping the front legs. Use your hand to measure (see text above), and mark the lines carefully with chalk. Then clip along the lines.

Marking and clipping hind leg lines. Mark the lines carefully with chalk. Then clip along the lines.

The blanket clip

This clip is useful for any animal who works hard but who is thin skinned or in need of extra protection over the vulnerable area of the loins. Enough hair should be removed to prevent loss of condition.

The blanket-clipped horse must be stabled at night and needs almost the same care as the full or hunter-clipped horse. He has a little more protection from the cold and will not need a quarter sheet while being exercised.

Before clipping, chalk the blanket shape on the horse's body with the saddle fitted. Use the bottom of the saddle flap as a guide for how low the bottom line of the 'blanket' should lie. The shape must be level and must match on all sides. Make the corner of the 'blanket' curved, not square. Mark and clip the leg lines as described on page 19.

THE BLANKET CLIP – a 'blanket' of coat is left on the back, loins and rump, while the head, neck, shoulders and belly are clipped. Leaving half the head unclipped is optional.

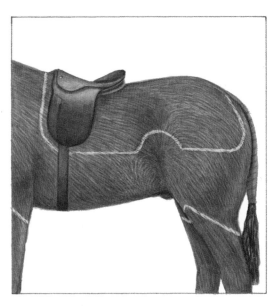

Draw the blanket shape with the saddle fitted. The lower blanket line should be straight except for a shallow semi-circle over the stifle.

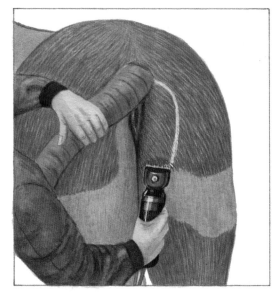

The blanket clip from the rear. Hair under the dock is being clipped. A bandage keeps the tail out of the way. When the tail is lying flat, a clipped strip will show either side.

Trace clips

This clip is so called because it was first used on harness horses who were clipped to the height of the traces. The trace clip is a good compromise for horses and ponies. They are able to work hard at weekends and during the holidays without undue stress or loss of condition, and can usually live outdoors for part or (if hardy) even all of the time. The trace clip's traditional shape is sometimes modified to suit animals who sweat in slightly different areas. The chaser clip is a high trace clip with the animal's head also clipped.

Horses with chaser or high trace clips must be stabled indoors at night, wear rugs, and receive regular care. Hardy native breeds with very low trace clips are usually able to live outdoors day and night. Consider the work your horse will be doing and use your common sense to decide how high to trace-clip him – see page 24 for more variations. The time that he will be able to spend outdoors depends on the following:

1. The height and shape of the trace clip.

2. The type of horse and the thickness of his winter coat.

3. The time of year and the behaviour of the weather.

4. The availability of correctly fitting New Zealand rugs. (Ideally one to wear and one to air!)

5. The amount of supplementary food being fed.

THE HIGH TRACE CLIP. Here the head and legs are unclipped but the horse will be able to work hard. The clip looks neat and purposeful. It is particularly useful for head-shy individuals.

THE MEDIUM TRACE CLIP. This traditional trace clip is the true compromise: the horse benefits from being clipped where he sweats the most but retains his winter coat on the top half of his body.

Trace clips cont.

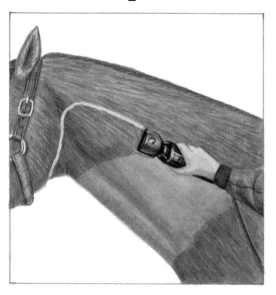

Decide how high you wish the clip to be on the neck and body. Draw the shape with chalk. Stand back to check how it will look. Then start to clip the neck.

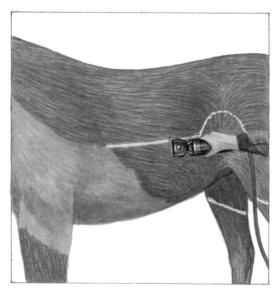

The trace line from shoulders to flanks is very long and noticeable. Take time and trouble to clip a straight line. It should not look ragged or moth-eaten.

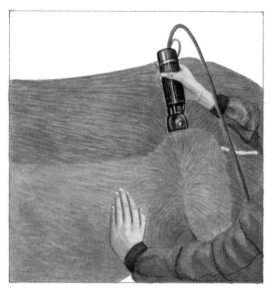

Clipping the stifle. Clip an arc shape over the stifle. Work against the lie of the coat. Here the finishing touches are being made. Clip lightly to avoid making 'clipping lines'.

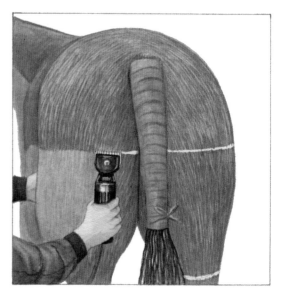

Clip to the chalk lines on the back of the hind legs. These must be level when viewed from behind. If the horse is stabled at night, you may follow the shape on page 20.

LOW TRACE CLIP   VERY LOW TRACE CLIP

Here the windpipe, chest, area between the
front legs, and lower parts of the shoulders
and belly are clipped. This is suitable for
horses who work hard occasionally.

A strip down the windpipe, widening on the
breast, going between the front legs and
under the belly, is quick to clip. Hardy types
may 'live out' overnight, with a NZ rug.

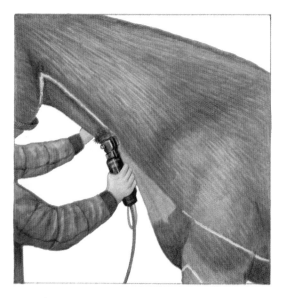   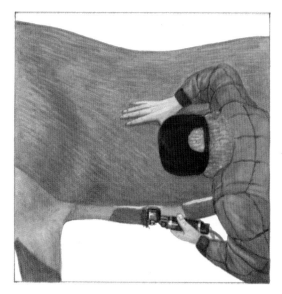

For the low trace clip, chalk the guide-line,
then clip under the neck up to the throat and
the chest to the points of the shoulders. Clip
between the lines on the forearm.

Clipping the belly line. Chalk a line on both
sides, from the elbows to the stifles. Clip
between the front legs. Clip the belly up to
the lines, taking extra care in the genital area.

Customised clips

The clipping style can be adapted to suit the indiviudal needs of your horse and pony. With experience you will know where your horse sweats up, and will be able to decide how much coat to remove and from where. Here are a few more clips to give you ideas.

The bib clip, for example, would suit a pony who is ridden infrequently and who sweats on his neck and chest when worked. The apron clip would also suit an animal in very light work but will give some additional protection to the belly – which may be appreciated by horses or ponies who like to lie down or roll in wet mud.

You may even want to personalise a clip by leaving a small motif, such as a diamond, star, or heart shape, somewhere on the horse's coat. Provided you don't get carried away (and the horse is not being shown) this can add a touch of fun to your clipping.

BIB CLIP

APRON CLIP

IRISH CLIP

IRISH CLIP WITH HALF HEAD REMOVED

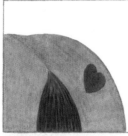

Just for fun – a heart-shaped motif left unclipped on a child's pony

In winter, freeze-brand marks can be clipped so that they are not lost beneath a thick coat.